To Denise,
Hope (
poems!

salmonpoetry

Publishing Irish & International
Poetry Since 1981

Anne Lannan.

Tides Shifting Across My Sitting Room Floor

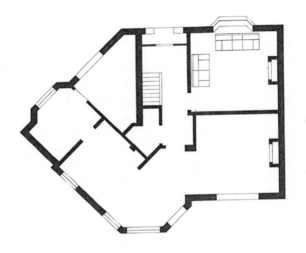

ANNE TANNAM

Published in 2017 by
Salmon Poetry
Cliffs of Moher, County Clare, Ireland
Website: www.salmonpoetry.com
Email: info@salmonpoetry.com

ISBN 978-1-910669-79-2

COVER IMAGE: 'Seascape' by Karen Pleass at Swinky Doo
COVER DESIGN & TYPESETTING: Siobhán Hutson
TITLE PAGE IMAGE: 'Houseplan' by Aislinn Murphy
Printed in Ireland by Sprint Print

Salmon Poetry gratefully acknowledges the support of
The Arts Council / An Chomhairle Ealaíon

For Elizabeth Tannam (nee o'Loughlin)

1929–2013

'*We are our stories. We tell them to stay alive*
or keep alive those who only live now in the telling.'

NIALL WILLIAMS 'History of the rain'

Acknowledgements

Thanks to the editors of the following publications or websites in which some of the poems, or versions of the poems, first appeared:

A New Ulster, All The Worlds Between, Bare Hands, Blue Max Review, Boyne Berries, Census, Crannóg, fathers and what must be said, Flare, Episteme, Headspace, HeadStuff, Irish Literary Review, Literature Today, Ofi Press Magazine, Poethead, Poetry Bus, Poetry Ireland Review, Prairie Schooner, Upstart, The Stinging Fly & Skylight47.

Thanks to all my wonderful co-writers at Dublin Writers' Forum and a special shout out to the amazing band of fellow writers, family and friends who helped push each draft towards a cohesive collection: Liz Barron, Fióna Bolger, Alvy Carragher, Katie Dwyer, Johanna Hally, Frank Jordan, Colm Keegan, Alison Kingston, Eithne Lannon, Jennifer Little, Phil Lynch, Éamon Mag Uidhir, Claire Murphy, Liz McSkeane, Donal Tannam, Gerard Tannam, Vivian Tannam, Patricia Verling & Dimitra Xidous.

Thanks to Jessie and Siobhán at Salmon Poetry for inviting me to swim with the fishes.

Finally, thanks to Neil, Claire, Aislinn, Sian and Darragh for putting up with me. A poet is a strange creature to find in your home.

Contents

Airborne

Wind gathered up the smell of the sea,
carried it here three miles away.
I can feel shells crunch under my feet,
shingle and sand between my toes,
boats are sailing, tides are shifting
across my sitting room floor.

At Sea

I'm watching a film. There's a scene at the end
where the leading lady gets into her car and drives.
The camera—a bird's eye view of highways and roads—
follows her progress, until the journey slows,
curves along the edge of sunshine and sea,
before braking to standstill on gravel and sand.

I've seen this film before. A light-hearted affair,
no hidden meaning or sudden twist at the end.
But this time I'm sitting on the couch, trying not to cry,
wondering why the sight of the ocean at the end of a film
feels like someone close just died.

As the credits roll, I let the waves run in to shore
until my breathing calms and I am more myself again,
forty-six years old and counting,
acknowledging the sadness
of continents and planets unexplored,
of a single self who got side-tracked early.

I think of childless friends
who speak of emptiness and longing,
the inconsolable sea inside
and that defining moment,
whether through age or circumstance,
when only one reality remains and grief shows up
to fill the void.

Family Census

Four live births
nine pregnancies
one stopping at four months
my father wrapping
the contents in newspaper
to bring downstairs for disposal.

On the final pregnancy
blood clots the size of a fist
the doctor saying *I think you've lost it*
and you—hands cupped
about my heart—refusing to let go.

Eden 1

When I was small
God was my mother's face
my father's lap
a trinity of brothers
to protect me.

There was some sadness
in the garden
but fruit hung low
and I had arms and hands
to reach and pluck
an open mouth
eager for sweetness.

Mobile Library

When I was sick
books came to me

in the arms of my father.
He'd stick his head

around the door
ask how I was

perch his large frame
at the end of my bed

pull out books
hidden in coat pockets

place flying carpets
within my reach.

Comfort Eating

The story of a story
in a book on a shelf
took it down

women who ran with wolves
a girl with red dancing-shoes

a bluebearded villain
keys dripping blood
hands and feet and heads
chopped off

dolls in pockets
Baba Yaga
her swirling whirling
copper cauldron

underworlds
low-hanging pears
in darkened gardens
on moonless nights

lonely skeletons
entangled in nets
bodies sung whole

yes bodies sung whole

I ate it up
licked the plate
asked for more.

At the Zoo

I'm smiling at the camera wearing
a jumper you knitted. You're smiling too,
but holding your handbag like it feels too heavy,
like the time I got lost by the Seal Enclosure
—when crowds hid your familiar shape—
running past the polar bears, the penguins,
the elephants, frantic for a glimpse of your coat,
your handbag, your mammy outline amongst these strangers,
until finally we found each other by the Bat House, tearful,
strained by the separation, the afternoon unsteady around us.

The Long Wait

Just today—out of the blue—
my eighty-eight-year-old father said
I am very proud of you.
A five-year-old heart
listening inside
my middle-aged chest
skipped a beat
pumped for joy.

I never knew
it was patiently waiting
to hear the sound
come round again
of long-legged races
in our back garden
where my childhood lived
happily ever after
before we moved on.

Unfinished Business

On their wedding day his father said
I'll forgive you everything if you do right by this girl:
the unfinished education;
the empty table setting at Christmas;
the family name unpolished, unloved.

I never met my grandfather,
a man who lived under the glare of his wife,
but I remember my grandmother—a small woman—
her mouth eternally disappointed.
Dad bringing us down to visit her
to the small dark house on Bulfin Road
where the furnishings took themselves too seriously.

Later, in that same house, I found a studio photograph
of the polished family; my grandfather, something familiar
in the way he's leaning against the table,
my dad, a beautiful child about three years old
sitting beside his brothers and sisters, and there
my grandmother, upright and disapproving
staring into the camera, daring it to blink.

That blond-haired little boy,
the man who loved his wife for sixty years,
couldn't wait to cycle home from work,
gave up his wages every week,
cooked our fry on Saturday mornings,
scrubbed our nails, polished our shoes.

Still wonders if he did enough.
Still wonders if he's been forgiven.

When We Go Shopping

When we go shopping, just the two of us
—Mam in her eighties, me in my forties—
there's a silly game we like to play.

When we go shopping, just the two of us,
as we stand by the cashier waiting to pay,
Mam says *If she* (meaning me)
doesn't behave, I'll cut her out of the will.
I stand there nonchalant, scanning the shelves
while the cashier busies herself giving back change,
pretending she didn't hear.

Another thing Mam likes to say
when we go shopping, just the two of us,
is *This young one here is my daughter.*
The cashier tries with all her might
to see the young girl, but all she can see
is grey hair and glasses, middle-aged me.

When we go shopping, just the two of us,
I get to be the child again, out with my mam for the day.
On the way home if we pass by sweets on display,
I'd really love to grab a few, but I never do
because I know she'll make me put them back.

Safety in Numbers

Yes I'm awake.

That's the signal.

Leave your fear behind,
race across the landing
to your sister's room,
tuck yourself
into the warm bed.

One small body,
two small bodies,
armed against the darkness.

Final Addition

Upstairs his sisters sleep
while we prepare
the sitting room for his arrival.

The midwife calls,
takes one look at my dilated pupils,
pronounces the party in full swing.

Off we go, the boy and I,
he headfirst, me on all fours,
two sides of the same contractions.

A primitive riot of sound,
the metallic smell of birth in the air,
our final hallelujah push,

and there he is,
breathing us in.

Your Children Are Not Your Children

The garden sprouts a sandbox in the shape of a green turtle,
a slide, a double swing, toys half-hidden in the grass.

A month of head lice crawling between four heads, fine-combing
in my sleep.

Let loose in a hayfield, small legs pumping happiness
until the allergy kicks in, slows his breath to shallow rasping,
forces his swollen eyes shut.

First day of a new school, searches for a familiar face,
her fingernails digging into the palm of my hand.

Against a backdrop of winter sunshine and loud shrieking,
well-wrapped bodies roll down sand dunes at Curracloe.

That moment when we walk past Smyths toy store, and no one
asks to go in.

They're at the kitchen table talking college, rents, where to buy a tent
for Electric Picnic, and all we hear are doors closing on empty bedrooms,
trains departing, planes taking off.

Parallel Universe

It happens unexpectedly.
I might be walking into town,
each house I pass in its rightful place,
neat rows of apartments all standing in line.
Then a gap appears, revealing space I'd missed before.
Another dimension opens wide
and my eyes travel down for the very first time
an astonishing, ordinary, small, side street

where—catching a glimpse of another reality—
I see people I don't know leading competent lives,
parking their cars outside well-tended gardens,
they move through their world
like it's always been there.

Sometimes I wonder if
as soon as I pass by—my footsteps
carrying me light years away—
might this other dimension, this unexplored country,
fade like an echo that passes through space

and the only world left will be this life I am living,
and the only route open this walk into town.

Feral
for T

I remember reading a story once,
set in Victorian England,
about a gentleman whose young wife
—in an unexplained miracle
of the very worst kind—
gradually turns into a fox.

And here you are sitting in our kitchen
at a quarter to one in the morning,
dressed in someone else's coat,
smelling of neglect and nights
without the comfort of sleep.

Are you well?
Such a useless question
when thirst is slowly unravelling summer
from your skin,
your hair,
your eyes,
from the corners
of your mouth.

We offer you the couch
but you are racing across fields,
Winter's cold breath pounding in your ears.

By Decree

I will not allow accidents in my kingdom.
In my kingdom there'll be no talk of what might've been prevented.

The word *heartbroken* for a thousand years I banish.
I banish messengers bringing news that breaks the heart.

There will be no blame in my kingdom.
In my kingdom no one will point the finger, no one will lay fault.

Sleeplessness will not take hold of the night-time.
Night-time will be free of the slow ticking clock.

Bodies laid out decades before their time, I forbid.
I forbid the stillness that gathers around the bodies.

I will not allow the aftermath to live in my kingdom.
In my kingdom the aftermath will not lay waste to the seasons.

Rift

I'm not myself today.
Or if I'm being honest
I am myself, just not the version
I want the world to see.

The self I am today
—this porous, fragile thing—
tries so hard to stay contained
while my appropriate self looks on

refusing to catch my eye.
Instead she goes about her business,
making sure the work gets done,
dogs are walked, bins put out.

I think she is afraid of me and the mess
I'll leave behind, and you just know
she'll be the one who'll have to
catch the falling pieces.

Groundhog Day

I laugh at 1950s woman
tied to the kitchen sink,
her hair in curlers, head filled
with cleaning products
and ways to please her husband
after his long day's work.

Yet sometimes,
lying awake
juggling roles,
adding items
to a never-ending list of tasks
to be completed,

I hear in the darkness
the kitchen sink
shuffling towards me

and her laughter
as she applies coral pink
lipstick to her smiling mouth.

So Much Better

I hear myself better
    talking with you.
Along lilypadded
    waterways
or deep and hushed
    in bluebelled woods
I see myself clearer
    out walking with you.

The world spins slower
    thoughts simplify
        resonate
          settle
            down
            flow
          again
      in easy
    conversation.
Planets realign.

Curled up on either
    side of the couch
listening to J.J. Cale
    his voice meandering
through gravel and silk
    I feel in tune.
The song of myself
    sounds so much better
when I sing it with you.

Thanksgiving

For the small things that blue our horizon
shine our sun, star our night sky,
like fruit, the ingenuity of skin and peel,
pip and pulp, and sweet, sweet juices.

Or duvets, pillows, clean warm sheets,
the quiet healing of a deep sleep,
that momentary release from the clamour of thought
and imagined limitations.

Let's look again at these glorious bodies of ours.
Tell me we're not all perfect
in our idiosyncratic beauty.

See here, seven stitches
gained twenty-eight years ago
cycling into an open van door.
When I touch the faded scar
I feel again the surgeon's hands
small and expert, gentle on my broken skin,
give thanks for the gift of his confident touch
and this unshaken body I'm still cycling in.

Breathe deeply in this moment,
name the miracle of who we are,
all we've lost, all we strive for, and give thanks
for our ocean crossing,
the sting of salt and wind,
waves that buffet and bruise,
bringing us closer to the driftwood shore
of open, painful, joyful living.

Listen Here, Australia!

Listen here, Australia!
We're willing to make a deal.
You can have her for a whole year.

Yes, I know, our generosity knows no bounds.
She's yours for the next three hundred and sixty-five days.

You mind her well, Australia,
treat her like family. Say to her
Welcome, our sister, our love,
sit with us a while, eat at our table,
feel the sun on your skin.

Show her your sights, Australia,
amaze her with your scale and size.
Woo her with history and song.
Make her fall a little in love
with your oceans, your rivers,
the wide and roving spaces in between.

Hold her close when night draws in.
Let the stars in your upside-down sky
shed for her vast continents of light.

Allow her space to simply be, Australia,
give her room to breathe and grow,
trees to lean on, friends for shelter,
a home from home to come back to
when her working day is done.
Lend her soft pillows, fresh, cotton sheets
to ease her journey into sleep.

Be good to her and she will seep
into your red soil and blossom you.

And when the time is right, Australia,
return her to us, be gracious when she packs to leave.
Hide gifts inside her homebound luggage:
a feather poised for flight,
a stone the colour of your eyes.

Testament

(i)

She keeps asking
why I don't write about her,
why poems about my father
come easily and naturally,
settling in on the page
like a comforting presence
so the world can see at a glance
the strong, clean lines of lifelong love.
She trawls my poems for evidence
of a daughter's love,
comes up empty-hearted every time.

So I write this poem for her,
begin at the very beginning
in case I stumble if I try to jump on
when the memories are already moving.

A cot in the corner of their bedroom.
I lie quietly, listening for her footsteps,
waiting for the rush of love she brings with her.
Now she comes, tucks me in, and bending over
kisses me and the world feels safe and warm,
but as she moves towards the door
she leaves a trace of her sadness behind.
It settles like dust on my bones.

Before I could pronounce the word,
I knew *mammy* meant *home*.

I knew *mammy* meant *tired*.

(ii)

I tumble out the school door
at home time. She's waiting,
her smile out-stretched to catch me.
We walk home together hand in hand.
I tell her all about my day.
It's funny how in the remembering
there's never any brother in sight,
the sky is always blue.
That memory, sweet and uncomplicated,
tells the whole truth; sometimes the word
mammy simply translates as *love*.

Other days, when least expected,
the atmospheric pressure changes.
Tap tap on the glass, tap tap on her mind,
where does the arrow point today?
A weather system moves in,
clouds gather across her sky.

Momentum building, energy rising,
she keeps herself busy with projects and tasks.
Busy, frantic into the night, it has to be finished,
it has to be right. Can no one else see
it has to be right?
Running on empty she deteriorates fast,
the barometer indicates *falling*.
Tap tap on the glass, tap tap on her mind,
where will the arrow point today?
Inside her head it feels like rain:
persistent, heavy, exhausting.

Weather-beaten,
she takes to the bed—the only
place of shelter she knows—
but she never leaves us for long.

I still miss her when she's gone.

(iii)

She lies in bed, unable to rise.
The sadness has returned;
this time it will not let her go.
Drained of energy and the will to get up
she lies there helpless as a child.
I put my head around the door to check on her,
to see if she's come back again but she's sleeping now,
a restless sleep that brings no peace.

Something stirs in me,
a subtle shift of sorts
catches my teenage body off balance.
I stumble across the threshold
heel over head, land feet first beside her bed.
Like Alice in Wonderland
our dimensions have changed.
I am big and she is small
in this strange, up-ended world.

I survey the room with new eyes:
tidy away what needs to be tidied,
tuck in the side of the sheet,
fold away my teenage years.
Through the looking glass I see
the child in her, the mother in me.

Troops are called in to save the day:
doctors with their expertise, offering advice
and pills that promise to numb the pain.
It takes a while to find the mix that matches
her needs as she tosses upon the waves
of a little dose of this might work,
or a little dose of that might do.
Finally the storm passes on,
leaves her feeling like her usual self,
almost—but not quite—as good as new.

Sleeves rolled up, apron tied,
she resumes the household duties
with her usual diligent care.
Everything seems as it should be,
only now the word *daughter*
feels heavy as stone,
mother as flimsy as air.

(iv)

These moments in time
preserved like scratches on an old LP
keep playing through my adult life,
the needle stuck in the deepening groove,
repeating, repeating, repeating

I want my mammy to be well.
I want her back to stay.
I want her to leave
that other child behind,
the one who kicks
and drags her down,
leaving her sad and far away.

If I become a mammy,
what if I'm unwell?
What if I can't stay?
Who will I be?
Where will I go,
if I am sad and far away?

I've been humming that tune for years.
Now that it's written down
I can hear another song
playing soft and low.
The music sounds the same,
an old, familiar feeling,
but the lyrics tell a story
never listened to before.

It's the story of a woman, a mother, a warrior
who never stops fighting, who never gives in.
Though exiled, lost and far from home,
she never gives up. She always comes back.

Is that enough to satisfy
the girl who lives inside
those memories ?

It's enough.

Love is more than a clumsy poem
or a weather front moving across the sky.
It's footfalls sounding on the stairs,
surmounting every step and turn,
a landing breached, a door pushed open,
the world is safe and warm.

Becoming Human

Two feet firmly on the ground
feel the steady earth beneath you.
Eyes wide, ears pricked
scan the horizon, plot your course
one foot in front of the other.
Never lose sight of your destination
but rest when darkness falls.
Stare up at the stars.

Put down what you're carrying
for a moment and listen.
This is important.
Press your thumb against
the fingers of the same hand.
Can you feel your nerve-ends
tingling, the muscles responding
your grip on what is possible, tightening?

Most likely an accident that first time
you smash stone against stone
at just the right angle.
A flake detaches, leaving a sharp edge.
Testing it with your finger, you draw blood
a trickle of red; salt and iron on stone.
Animals close by sniff the air
head for higher ground.

Flint and friction.
Remember these words.
They will lengthen the day
protect you from predators
roast a carcass until it falls
tender and succulent from the bone.
Tribes will rise up
from the flickering warmth.

You are not alone.
The world beyond your daily life
moves in and out of view.
Practise animal worship
anoint the dead with ochre
sprinkle the soil with semen and blood.
Breathe deeply, let your mind wander
feel the world expand.

Still gazing at the stars? Are you
ready to birth your night visions?
Dazzle us with images on clay
charcoal on cave ceilings, birds, beasts
swimmers moving across a desert sea.
Leave finger-prints, hand-prints
brush-strokes, a shout of colour,
the tantalising glimpse of personality.

Call every living creature to your side.
Label mountains, valleys, evergreens.
Number the seasons and the winds.
Open wide rivers, water cascades
language comes rushing through.
Sweeten your tongue with honey
and the earth will rise, stars will fall
yearning to taste your mouth.

Travelling the Distance

My uncle rings me from Canada
on the far side of the world
to tell me he's been up Near North
with a very good friend he met
at York University years ago.
They brought a copy of my poems,
sat beside the lake reading aloud
each syllable fresh-minted in the resin-scented air.

The story catches in my throat
and I am moved beyond words,
indebted to the muse
who finally found me willing
after years of mute distress.

Staunch

I've sat in the donor's clinic
twenty-nine times
in almost as many years,
left arm outstretched,
needle inserted into the vein
while I looked the other way.

Twenty-nine units of blood,
O positive,
same type as you.

Ten units
you've needed
since Christmas,
and it's still only January.

I do the maths
in my head.
I won't be able
to keep you alive.

Adrift

Do you remember the photograph?
A miniature island perched on a stony beach,
red frilled bikini, blue spade, sandy toes,
surrounded by an ocean of pebbles, seaweed, driftwood,
upturned face smiling, eyes on you, my mainland, my terra firma.

What I wanted to ask was this:
Do you remember the shapes of clouds passing overhead,
or the movement of boats drifting just beyond the camera's reach?

Seer

Just one eye—the right—
not weeping exactly
more a steady watering
barely requiring a tissue
or any attention at all.

In her mind she registers
the beginning of this
phenomenon coinciding
with the arrival
of the word *prognosis*.

She pushes the thought aside
though it still flickers
like an unwelcome image
burning her retina,
a premonition of things to come.

Clarification

But when exactly does the countdown begin?
Do we have a few minutes grace or does it start
the precise moment the words are spoken?

Will it wait till we've exited the car park,
easing into the flow of rush-hour traffic
anxious to be home in time for tea?

Can we choose the months?
February is miles too short
September, November, April and June
fly by a day too fast.

And if the end, six months to a year,
brings too much pain, far too many hours,
can we revise our carefully thought-out plans
or propose an alternative means
to accurately measure the distance?

Eden 2

Who will remember
the sound of thunder
the night I was born?

Mother of pearl buttons
on my communion dress,
the veil, the shoes,
a tomboy turned princess for a day?

Who will remember the trees in the garden?

And Cobh Was Cousins

The train to Cobh
—*We're nearly there!*
Dunkettle, Little Island, Cobh Junction,
Fota, Carrigaloe, Rushbrooke—
— *where the Allens live ...*
Cobh station, end of the line
— *Check under the seats before we go.*

11 Harbour Hill,
a marble step worn and warm,
Granny and Mammy inside
talking, smoking, taking no notice
— *Go on outside and play!*
The stag's head glaring in the hall
because Grandad liked to shoot
but he was dead before I was born.

Aunties who looked like Mammy but sounded different,
her voice different when she was with them,
talking, smoking, taking no notice
— *Go on outside and play!*
Dad on a bench reading the paper
the promise of 99s if we're good.

Dinnertime, big ones in the front room,
no one to mind them,
punching, laughing, planning danger,
small ones in the kitchen,
grown–ups taking no notice,
soggy fish fingers, mash and beans
— *Go down to Ellises' and play!*

Racing up to Auntie Maura's for our bath
because Granny only had one toilet out the back,
a chamber pot under our bed with flowers on the side
in case we had to pee at night.

A piano out of tune in the sitting room upstairs
— *Be quiet your granny is in bed with Gregory Peck!*
Outside the window a liner passes slowly,
then a smaller boat, another big one
— *The rain has stopped, go on outside and play.*

Older cousins, big brothers
climbing from the low road to the high
— *Don't try it you're too small!*
Fighting bullies on Lynch's Quay,
fishing for danger,
hanging off buildings,
taking the train to Cork on their own.

Mackerel are breaking
at the water's edge,
a tangle of rods
— *Stand back that hook will take your eye out!*
flashing in water,
hanging from hooks,
twitching in boxes,
blood and guts on the pier.

Trips to Cuskinny
around by the rocks if the tide is out
— *Can we stop in Hurleys for Cidona?*
— *My legs are tired.*
— *Are we nearly there?*
— *Stop whinging.*

Swimming in Whitepoint
— *Only go in as far as your waist!*
Mammy nearly drowned here when she was a girl.
Under the water, stones and seaweed,
rubber dollies on our feet.

Three weeks over
— *It won't be long until ye're back!*
— *Check under the beds before ye go!*
One last visit to the prom.
Backwards journey browner, taller,
cathedral bells still singing in our ears.

Hidden Treasure

To locate,
gently cup
the back
of a grown
man's head.

Slowly,
so as not to
alarm him,
move your hand down
over bony ridges,
unyielding plains,
until heel and palm
sense a falling away.

Let fingertips
take over now,
obeying curve
and inclination,
until they reach
the hollowed
tender spot
where he sleeps
cradling
his boyhood dreams.

Jazz

doesn't have to shout
throw shapes flash colours
I *pot of gold* his rainbow contours
trace them with my fingertips

doesn't have to song and dance
for me to sway and sashay
to his rhythm anytime
softly rising steady beat

doesn't have to butterfly
peacock strut cockatoo
to capture flutter lightly lightly
trembling feathers breathless wings

Seven Signs of Love

AGE 22

— A declaration of flowers at the airport
— The gift of an inscribed fountain pen
— Letters written on both sides of the page and posted
  the next morning
— The sound of the telephone ringing at precisely bang
  on the button
— The song *The First Time Ever I Saw Your Face*
— Table for two
— The world inside one sleeping bag

AGE 44

— Bicycle repaired
— Precious files thought lost forever, retrieved
— The smell of barbecued food coming in the kitchen
  window
— The question *How was your day?*
— Two chairs beside a hospital bed
— Table for six
— The world inside a sleeping house

By Numbers

In the last weeks of pregnancy,
wide eyed, rotund and impatient,
I'd fill the fridge with yogurts, cheeses,
cold meats, wondering if I'd be a mother
before the food reached its *sell by* date.

Staring at those mystical numbers
gave me comfort, reduced the unknown
to an ordered sequence of events.
If the date passed I need only replace the item
to keep the world from spinning off its axis.

Years later, hurtling through space
without the safety net of *best before*,
poring over your medical charts,
analysing numbers on a page,

I've become an expert.
I, who never understood
statistics or algebra,
have taken to measuring rotations,
seasons, other worlds.

Reframe

I head over to visit you.
You've spent the night in hospital,
platelets so low you bled
just for the heck of it.

We don't panic anymore, do we?
Like in the beginning,
when the sight of runaway blood
prompted illegal U-turns
racing back to St James's Hospital.
Stay calm, stay calm, keep pressure on it.

I head over to visit you.
The dog has eaten your bottom teeth.

Tired of chocolates still in their wrappers,
hearing aids, pin cushions and rubbish from the bin,
he was tempted by your teeth instead.
You're left with half a smile,
someone else's blood inside you,
coursing through your stubborn veins.

That silly dog, lying on the couch.
Butter wouldn't melt in his mouth.
We're all laughing:
you and me and Dad.

I'm wondering is this as far from dying
as we can hope to be?

All Fall Down

I've been clearing out.
You handed me a bag full of pocket tissues,

twenty or more packets, some unopened,
most with one or two missing in action.

I took them home, along with the gloves and scarves
you knew you wouldn't need again,

and we took to using them
like the stash would last forever,

down the bottom of school bags, swimming bags,
jacket and coat pockets.

We took to using them
like they could be replaced

when the last one went missing.

Final Instructions

When the time comes
no need to stand around
an open grave
eyeing the sky
for signs of rain.

You believe in a God
who can turn water into wine,
sinners into saints,
ashes into risen bodies.

And while we're waiting
for the last day, we can use
your green-fingered ashes
to fertilise the roses,

wrap your straight-talking
in a pink and gold urn,
stow it on a flight
crossing the Atlantic sea,

scatter the rest
down South at the mouth
of the harbour,
the islands in the background,
the cathedral playing your song.

Land's End

Week in, week out you've come to sit
in the lilac armchair, hold out your arm,
receive the rush of blood—
a levee to stem the incoming tide.

This week's results are back.

It no longer matters how fast we carry
sandbags, pack them tight,
hold our breath—
water is seeping through.

The nurse asks you how you're feeling.
Your eyes, trained now on the horizon,
take in the solemn sweep of harbour,
the blur of sea and sky.

Her words, the curl of the shore,
the weight of the land, receding;
a siren call—low, hypnotic—
thrumming through your veins.

Me & Bobby McGee

When the others left
I stayed behind,
sat weeping by your side,
a child again, entreating you to stay,
until your stillness entered me.
And slipping my hand under your body
to where your warmth still lingered,
I sat with you a short time longer,
while outside the door
life without you waited to begin.

A friend called round to pay her respects,
asked me when you took your last breath,
did I feel the spirit or soul or whatever we call it
leave your body, and where did I think you are now?
I said when you took your last breath I felt you dissipate.

Now you are nowhere.

Now you are everywhere.

The crib you made still sitting on the TV stand,
three wise men looking towards the sky,
searching for a star to guide them,
Joseph with his arm around his pregnant wife,
a puzzled look on his knitted brow.

A few days after, I turned the dial to Sunshine 101.
Kris Kristofferson singing
Me and Bobby McGee,
words and music filling the car
until there wasn't any room left to breathe.

A week later you turned up in my dreams.
I think we spoke to one another
but neither of us knew what to say
before the dream moved on without you.

Still Not

still not sorting through clothes
still not dictating letters
still not giving dad the final hug
still not holding on
still not coming back

Downhill Fast

A dog with a bone,
my mind takes a phrase,
attaches it to images of you
during those final days.

I'm struck by the power of the mind
to go where it needs to go,
to write what needs to be written
over and over and over again,

until the story of your death
becomes a well-trodden path
through fine-powdered snow.

That First Year

The world spun on—
same rotation from West to East,
same speed, same seasons
in the same order.

Tides did their usual thing,
waves made their lapping sounds,
seagulls screeched their indignation.

Over in No. 80
small changes were noted:

the kitchen table
listing to one side,

no back and forth
of a conversation
sixty years
in the making.

Elsewhere:

the faint sound of
uillean pipes,
slide guitars,
pianos playing
traditional laments,

and Louis Armstrong
having to remind us
it's a wonderful world.

Undressing

Smaller items
he places on the bedside locker:

who came to visit this afternoon,
the name of his second eldest son.

Leaning down, he removes
the colour of his wife's eyes,

their honeymoon on the Isle of Man,
the last two years before she died.

Slowly he unbuttons
brother, husband, father, son,

slips them under the pillow
for safekeeping,

pulls back the covers,
turns out the light.

For They Shall Be Comforted

The only time I heard my father cry
was when his dog died.
He'd returned from the vet, was at
the kitchen sink, shoulders hunched,
hands trailing in the soapy water.
She was such a lovely little thing.

Yesterday we had our family pet put down,
the house on our return hollow with her absence.
Today I visited Dad, found him dozing in the sitting room
with the other residents, sat by his side,
stroked his arm, felt the urge to wake him,
tell him about the grace of her final movement,
head lowering to rest on her paws.

Five-year-old Jessie Comes to Visit

Striped tights, furry boots,
t-shirt stretched over her belly
announcing to the world
Laughing Girls Are Prettiest.

Arms and legs and shimmy hips
obeying the moves she's seen on TV.
Now she's Katie, now she's Taylor,
swiftly racing down the hall

past the wheelchairs, past the walkers.
Now she's racing back again,
stomping, twirling, pirouetting—amazing
the audience who sit in a circle around

her dance floor, bodies cupped
to catch the sparks flying from her feet.

Eden 3

I open my eyes and there
in the garden a lemon tree
blossoms, colour and fragrance
filling my senses.

Soon there will be fruit,
the comfort of the universe
resting in the palm of my hand.

And Again

A long, grey, endless beach, grey overhead,
grey beneath feet, and in the distance—just out of range—
the wind-thrown voices of others.

Time to begin again.

When the tide retreats a little, hunker down
with tools laid out: bucket, spade and coarse-grained sand,
shells and stones to decorate.

Castle upon castle, the beach fills up, monuments to hours
spent crouching. Avenues of shell-decked streets
invite the sun to part the clouds and briefly, as the grey divides
and light escapes across the sand, a city of fleck and gold
appears, slivers of silver and dazzling white,
shivers of colour reflecting the light.

The waters, lapping their applause, move further back
to grant the vision scope and space.

A moment please, to let the eyes drink in the scene,
to let the memory sink and settle, before the waters
change their mind and edge towards the falling-down.

Time to let go again.

Gather up the well-worn tools and shake the sand
from knees and hands, stretching aching muscles.
The empty-handed wind dies down and the others
drift along the beach, moving silently out of view.
No one turns to watch the tide perform its lonely duty.

A long, grey endless beach, grey overhead,
grey beneath feet, and nothing to fear
but salt and rain and pillars and pillars of sand.

South Wall

We walked the full length,
sat on rocks,
backs to the lighthouse,
gazed out at the lazy sea.

The air hummed dusk and evening,
water turning from gloss to satin, then matt,
sky and breath descending.

Headed back in silence
footfalling into the arms of Dublin Bay,
its familiar outline softening,
night a short car journey away.

Rise

Dare we let go
of all the things
we lost in the fire?
You are still breathing.
I am still breathing.
The Lighthouse still stands
at the far end of our South Wall.

And just today on the canal
twenty swans or more
took sudden flight
their wings
low and heavy
gathering speed
over startled waters.

Passers-by stopped
in their tracks, mesmerised,
and for one weightless moment
forgot they could not fly.

ANNE TANNAM is a page and performance poet from Dublin. Her first collection of poetry *Take This Life* was published in 2011 by WordOnTheStreet. Her work has appeared in literary magazines in Ireland and abroad and has featured on RTE Radio's Arena and on local radio. She has performed at literary events and festivals across Ireland including Lingo, Electric Picnic, Cúirt, Over The Edge, Ó Bheál, Word Jungle and Blackwater International Poetry Festival. Anne is co-founder of the weekly Dublin Writers' Forum and has been the featured reader at literary events across Ireland including the Sunflower Sessions, Monday Echo, Staccato, Mixed Messages, Glór, Stanzas, Tongue Box, Merg Sessions, Flying South, Dublin's Underground Beat & Dublin Indie Spirit. In October 2016 Anne was writer-in-residence at Chennai Mathematical Institute in India.